MEGA
colouring

PaRragon

Bath · New York · Singapore · Hong Kong · Cologne · Delhi
Melbourne · Amsterdam · Johannesburg · Shenzhen

First published by Parragon in 2014
Parragon
Chartist House
15–17 Trim Street
Bath BA1 1HA, UK
www.parragon.com

ISBN 978-1-4723-4086-3

Printed in China

Lightning dreams of winning the Piston Cup.

He is in the lead, but Chick Hicks is catching up!

The race is not only a draw ...

...it's a three-way tie!

The reporters love Lightning McQueen.

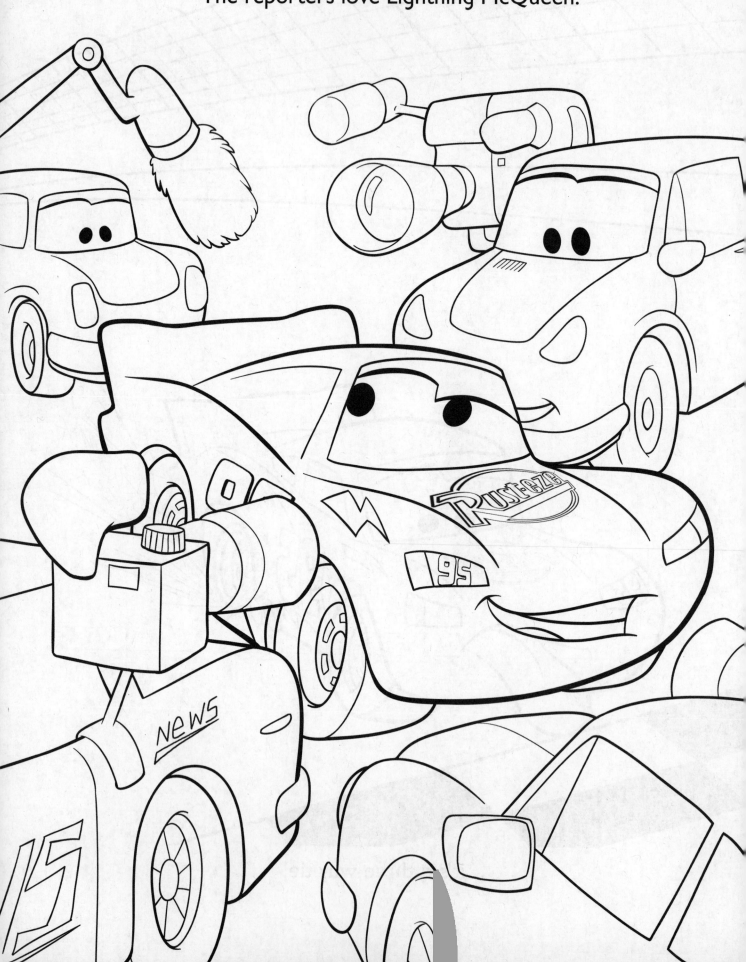

The King gets ready for the tie-breaker race.
It will be held in Los Angeles.

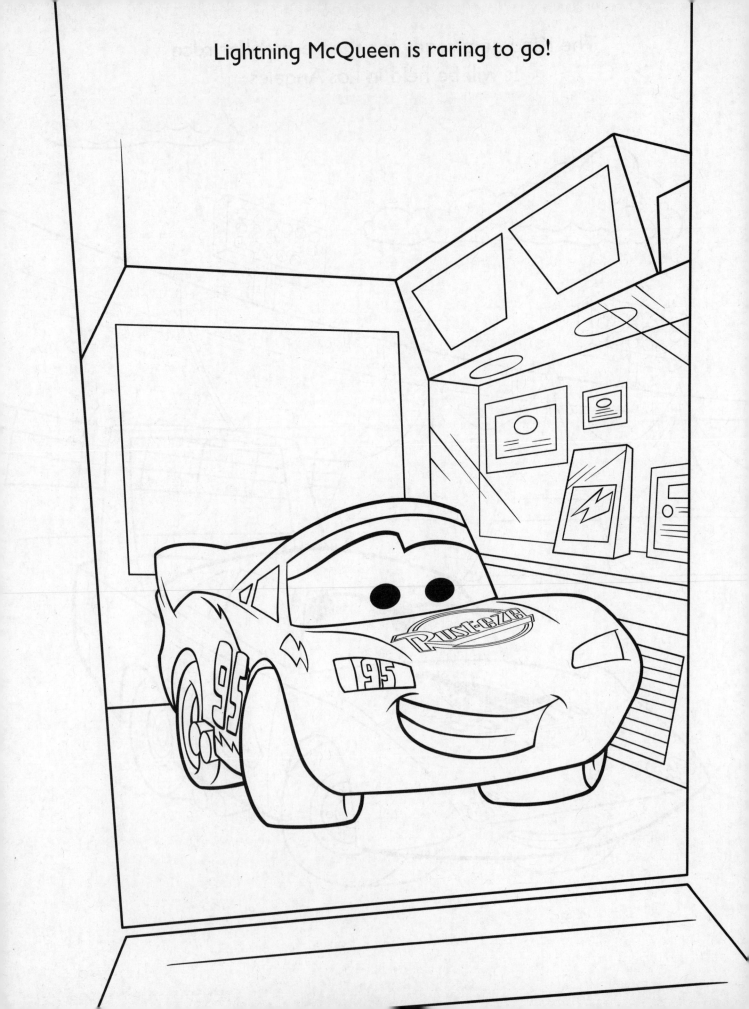

Lightning McQueen is raring to go!

Mack tries to stay awake on the long drive as he carries
Lightning to California.

The street racer, Snot Rod, is trying to bump Mack off the road.

Oh, no! Lightning has been knocked out of Mack's trailer.

Lightning crashes into a small town called Radiator Springs.

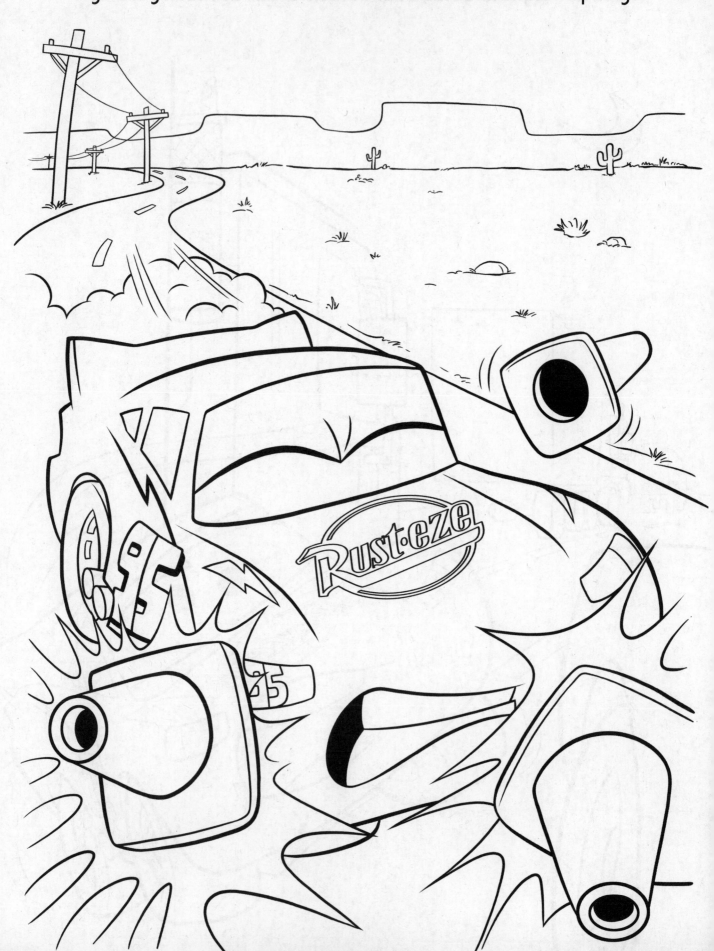

The local Sheriff is furious that Lightning has destroyed the road and got caught in a telephone wire.

Mater, the tow truck, comes to the rescue!

Lightning gets locked up for his bad behaviour.

There are many interesting characters in this town.
Lizzie is a little old car with lots of opinions.

Sarge is a strict army Jeep and Fillmore is a hippie Volkswagon.
They are unlikely friends.

Sally is a beautiful Porsche and the town lawyer.

She convinces the town to make Lightning stay and fix the road.
Sally and Lightning become good friends.

Lightning has to pull old Bessie to pave the new road.

Doc is an old racing champion who teaches Lightning there is more to racing than winning.

Lightning does not like this hard work, but it teaches him a lesson.

Guido is an Italian forklift who can change a flat tyre in four seconds!

Luigi runs the local tyre shop. He and Guido become important members of Lightning's pit crew.

Andy's best friend, and best toy, has always been a sheriff doll called Woody.

But then Andy gets a new Buzz Lightyear doll for his birthday.
Being a space ranger is cool!

Woody is jealous of Buzz. The two rivals argue
with each other and get lost.

Oh, no! Andy's neighbour, Sid, has got Woody and Buzz.
Sid is known as the toy-torturer.

Woody and Sid's other toys work together to save Buzz, who has a rocket strapped to his back.

Andy is moving house. Woody and Buzz need to catch up with the moving truck.

RC comes to the rescue. Woody and Buzz use the
rocket to launch themselves to Andy.

Buzz and Woody are back where they belong.

Woody and Buzz are now best friends.
Andy loves to play with them both.

Woody has been toy-napped! Al from Al's Toy Barn
steals him for his collection.

Woody used to be part of a show called *Woody's Roundup* with Jessie the cowgirl and Bullseye the horse.

Buzz and the gang head out to save Woody.
They use traffic cones to get safely across the road.

Stinky Pete does not want to go back into storage,
so will not let Woody leave.

Andy's toys dazzle Stinky Pete to help
Woody, Jessie and Bullseye escape.

The toys are free and head back to Andy's house.
He now has two new toys!

Years go by and Andy is all grown up and heading to college.
He puts Buzz and the toys in storage bags.

Woody is going to college with Andy. He is shocked when Andy's mum mistakes the other toys for rubbish.

Woody must save his friends before they get put in the rubbish truck.
Too late!

Phew! The toys have escaped. They think Andy does not want them so they head to a daycare centre.

Lotso the bear runs Sunnyside Daycare.
He welcomes Buzz and the other toys.

Woody tries to convince his friends that Andy did not get rid of them. They won't believe him, so he leaves.

The toys are excited to be played with again but the little children are too rough.

Lotso and his gang are mean and won't let Buzz and the toys move into the big kid room.

Woody finds out that Lotso is not very nice, so comes back to save his friends.

The toys escape through the rubbish chute. They need to run quickly to avoid being crushed.

The toys are safe and back at Andy's.
Woody prepares to say goodbye to his friends.

Woody realizes he does not want to leave his friends. He gets
Andy to donate all of his toys to a nice little girl named Bonnie.

Sulley is the number one Scarer at Monsters, Inc.

Mike is his best friend and partner. Sulley scares children and Mike collects their screams for power.

Fellow Scarer, Randall is always up to no good.
He is jealous of Sulley and Mike's scaring record.

One night, after everyone else has gone home,
Sulley finds a door that has not been put away.

Oh, no! A child has come through the door to Monstropolis.
Monsters think children are dangerous.

Sulley takes the little girl home. He and Mike try
to decide what to do with her.

Mike and Sulley sneak Boo back to Monsters, Inc. to send her home.
But sneaky Randall is there waiting.

Sulley and Mike try to escape.

Mr Waternoose is mad because Sulley has brought a kid into the monster world. He and Randall grab Boo ...

... and Mr Waternoose sends Sulley and Mike into the human world.

Mike is worried they will never get home. A Yeti tells them there is a nearby village for them to make their escape.

Mike, Sulley and Boo escape and run away from Randall.

Mike and Sulley want to get Boo back to her door.
Randall chases them through lots of doors.

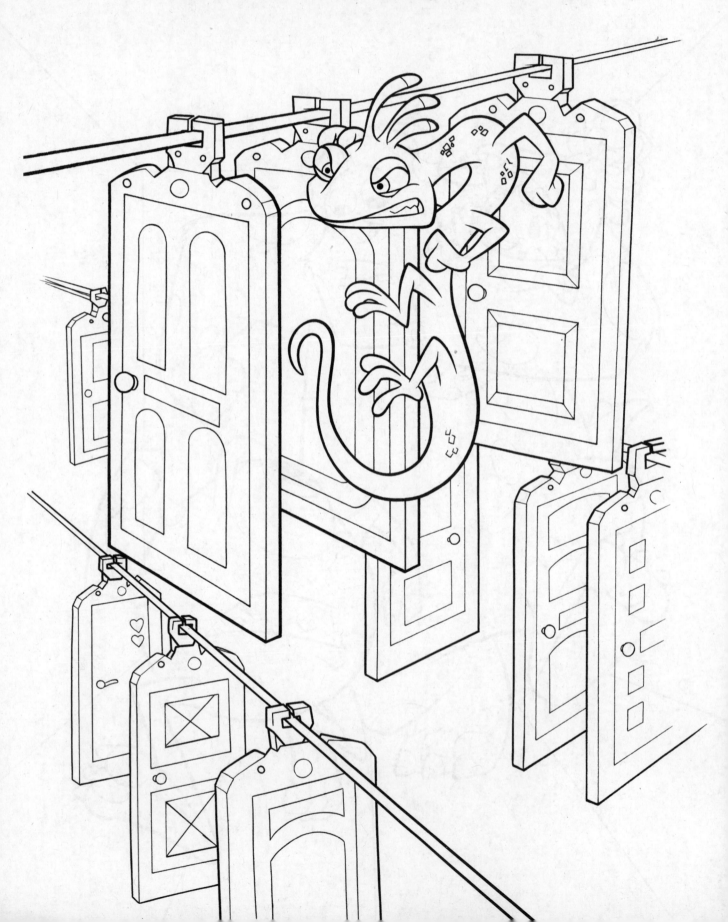

Hooray! Sulley and Mike send Randall to the human world.

Mr Waternoose is in big trouble for helping Randall.
The CDA take him away.

Boo is finally home in her own room. Sulley is sad to say goodbye.
The door to Boo's room is destroyed.

Mike is grown-up and ready for college! He's going to his dream school: Monsters University.

James P. Sullivan, or Sulley for short, is also a scare student.
He's one of the coolest monsters on campus!

The Oozma Kappas are a happy group of monsters.

The Oozma Kappas are a happy group of monsters.

Sulley cheers on the MU team at the football game
while Mike continues to study.

Mike and Sulley race against each other.

Mike and Sulley leave university for new adventures!

Marlin is a clownfish who lives in an anemone with his son, Nemo.

It's Nemo's first day of school, but Marlin is worried
that his son will not be safe.

Marlin was right! Nemo gets taken by a human diver.

Marlin is terrified and determined to find his son.
He asks other fish for help but they are too busy.

Finally, a forgetful blue tang named Dory agrees to help.
But she leads him into trouble with a shark!

Dory and Marlin find the scuba diver's mask.
They hope it holds a clue to where Nemo is.

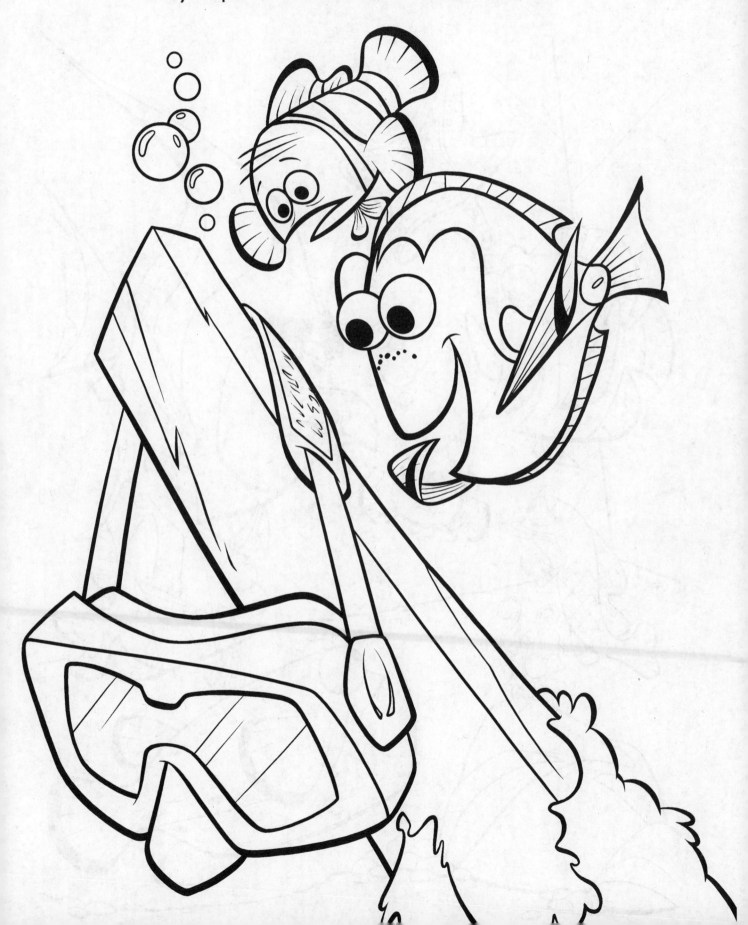

Meanwhile, Nemo finds himself in a dentist's fish tank with some friendly exotic fish.

Marlin holds off a scary anglerfish while Dory
reads the address on the mask.

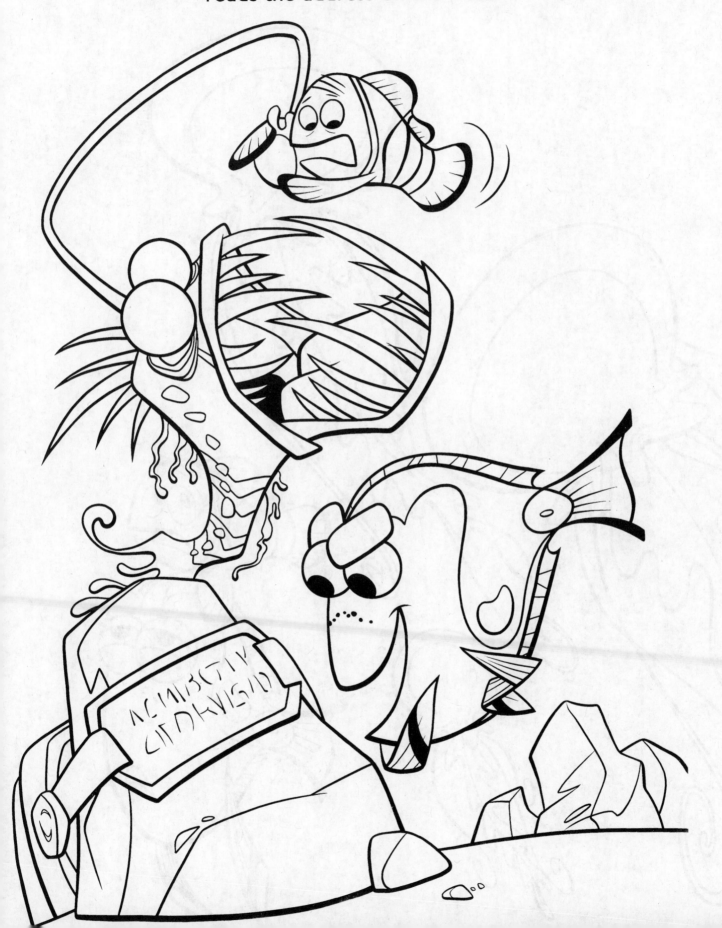

Marlin and Dory get caught in a sea of jellyfish. Dory is badly stung.

Nemo's new friend Gill teaches him how to block the filter in the tank so they can escape. But poor Nemo gets stuck!

The fish save Nemo and comfort him. Gill will not ask
Nemo to try the plan again.

Marlin and Dory get help from some Australian sea turtles.
They are cool dudes.

Nigel the pelican tells Nemo that his dad is on his way.

With the news of his dad coming to save him, Nemo is determined to escape. He tries Gill's escape plan again.

Nigel picks up Marlin and Dory from the harbour
and takes them to Nemo.

Gill flips Nemo into the spit sink, and Nemo
goes down the drain and into the ocean.

Marlin and Nemo are reunited at last. Hooray!